WORDWORKING
A PUNDEMIC

ROD HULME

 FriesenPress

One Printers Way
Altona, MB R0G 0B0
Canada

www.friesenpress.com

Illustrated by Paul Schultz

ISBN
978-1-03-915086-7 (Hardcover)
978-1-03-915085-0 (Paperback)
978-1-03-915087-4 (eBook)

1. HUMOR, PUNS & WORD PLAY

Distributed to the trade by The Ingram Book Company

To Bryce

Happy birthday!
Rod Hulme.

WORDWORKING

A PUNDEMIC

Introduction

Dear Reader,

You may recall this children's joke:
Q. *If a piggy gets a bruise, what do you use?*
A. *Oinkment.*

It's hard to resist a smile, isn't it? I created the puns in this book by changing a letter or two at a time just as in the joke above, although I trust that you'll find them somewhat more mature. The puns are worded as definitions rather than jokes. While this sort of wordplay is very common and some of the entries will surely have been coined already elsewhere, I've had fun devising the puns that you'll see in these pages. You can find many more examples of this sort of thing in *The Washington Post*'s regular contests.

Enjoy the collection! I hope you won't find too many examples that are overly subtle or obscure (or outdated, like their author). But I would ask you to give each entry its due consideration and not to speed through the pages too quickly—please don't *gobbledebook.*

Dedication

This book is dedicated to the memory of my parents, Peggy and Frank Hulme. They were both great readers who were sensitive to words and were quick to laugh. They appreciated clever turns of phrase, especially if they expressed wry humour, irony or similar mischief. At times my mother would use a posh English accent to act out a witticism that she came across, and the comments that my father wrote on the backs of our old photographs are still good fun to read. I like to think that Mom and Dad would have enjoyed this book very much.

All proceeds from the sale of this book will be donated to Diabetes Canada, a national health charity working to improve the quality of life for all people living with diabetes, through education, advocacy and research, and to Wellspring Stratford, an organization which offers supportive programming and resources to individuals affected by cancer and their caregivers, at no cost.

Cats and Dogs

A tabby at top speed - CATAPELT

The result of too much catnip - ODDIPUSS

Lions and tigers - LEOPARDKIN

A dog pound - BARKING LOT

Doggy scent - ODIE COLOGNE

Doggy disobedience - MUTTINY

Dog training - ROVERCORRECTION

A sniffer dog - LOCKER SPANIEL

When they see him, everyone says, "Aww!"- GUSHPUPPY

How dogs communicate - BARK CODE

Bowser's loudest sound - WOOFTOPS

A retriever, having run through the bushes
- BURRED DOG

Flora

A garden - SEAT OF YOUR PLANTS

Annuals - YEARLY RISERS

A tree trunk - WOODSTALK

Growing bonsai trees - SHORTICULTURE

Vegetables - FURROWFARE

Poison ivy - ITCHER PLANT

Success, for a Venus flytrap - INSECTINSIDE

Grass on the African plains - GNUTRITION

Fauna

Horses - NEIGHSAYERS

Where rabbits congregate - HAREABOUTS

How groundhogs live their lives - ON BURROWED TIME

Secure, for a baby marsupial - POUCHSAFE

A wolf's den - CUBHOUSE

Like a lonely buffalo - UNHERD-OF

Leviathan language - HUMPBACK WAILS

A sign of spring - HOMINGBIRDS

A bird's nest - THRUSHOLD

Soaring or squawking - GULLABILITY

Unlikely fate for a duck - EIDERDROWN

A mockingbird - STAND-IN AVIAN

A canary, compared to a condor - MINOR BIRD

Sounds at Halloween - SCREECH HOWLS

A cobra's fangs - VIPER BLADES

A shell - SNAIL'S PLACE

Voracious eel found in coral reefs - THAT'S A MORAY

Bees buzzing - HIVE TALKIN'

Bothersome insects bigger than black flies - YUSEEUMS

An extinction - GONE OF A KIND

A pair of binoculars - HUMBLE SPACE TELESCOPE

Science

A star - LIGHT WAY UP

The International Space Station - ASTROLAB

"I've made a great discovery!" - HALLEY'S COMMENT

Sir Isaac, compared to the rest of the family
- BIG NEWTON

Scotsman who developed the steam engine
- WATTSHISNAME

Einstein's reputation - FAME OF MIND

An oceanographer - WATERPROF

The destruction of the world's oceans - SEACIDE

An environmental activist who isn't Miss Thunberg
- PERSONA NON GRETA

"The Earth is flat." - COMIC BELIEF

Archaeology - SKULLDIGGERY

An archaeological find - SHINDUG

In Print

They're in the same genre - BOOK-ALIKES

The first few lines in Aesop's stories - FABLE SETTINGS

King Midas's state of mind - GILT-RIDDEN

Where *The Divine Comedy* was written
- DANTECHAMBER

Dialect in *Twenty Thousand Leagues Under the Sea*
- VERNEACULAR

Tweedledum and Tweedledee - ISODOPES

A novel set in the Old West - TEXBOOK

Like Tolkien's stories - INHOBBITED

There's one in every murder mystery - FIGUREDEAD

Where the body was found - 'NEATHCLIFF

Able to write poetry with either hand - IAMBIDEXTROUS

A collection of Edgar Allan's stories and poems
- POEPOURRI

Sending rhymes electronically - FAXING POETIC

An unusual thing for a Canadian phone book to do
- LACKSMITH

Church bulletins - PEWSLETTERS

A written reminder that could end up anywhere
- MEMORANDOM

Hackneyed writing - TRITE OF PASSAGE

A collection of bad jokes - CORNYCOPIA

Acronyms - MINUSSCRIPTS

A redacted version - COPYCUT

Editing or proofreading - TEXT MASSAGE

What proofreaders are like - TYPOCRITICAL

To speed-read - GOBBLEDEBOOK

Tattoos, often - WEARWORDS

A list of words that I've forgotten the meaning of
- LOSSARY

A postscript - SUBBLURB

History

Atlas carrying the world on his shoulders, for example
- MYTHILLOGICAL

What the Underworld was like -- INSULPHURABLE

The very first plough - PROTOTILLER

How Noah measured the planks for the ark
- INCUBITABLY

Old Testament skier - SLALOME

Yada yada yada - BABBLEON

Building the pyramids - TAPERWORK

Like Tutankhamun's surroundings - LUXORIOUS

How Cleopatra committed suicide - ASPLICATION

Cuneiform writing - PASTSCRIPT

Like actors in a play set in ancient Iran
- CAST AS PERSIANS

Why stand to attack the Gauls when you can ride
in comfort? - CHAIRIOT

A fleet of Roman galleys - OARMADA

A battleground - BLOODPLAIN

Castles - DUKEBOXES

A knight's armour - CLASH-ACTION SUIT

A medieval helmet - KNIGHTCAP

A siege strategy - MOATOCROSS

A foot soldier's life - WAR AND PACE

The peasant awakes - SERF'S UP

Like a monk's cell - HERMITICALLY SEALED

The rebuilding of London after the Great Fire
- WRENAISSANCE

"He's got a temper like Attila." - HUNPARALLELED

Before the invention of gunpowder - PREMUNITIONS

Weird guy who conquered Peru - FRANCISCO BIZARRO

Tropical Africa in colonial times - CONGOLOOTED

It was part of the Ottoman Empire - OLD TURKEY

Russia, for much of its history - TSARNATION

Heroic, like Horatio Nelson - ADMIRALBLE

"Don't forget the ice cream!"
- REMEMBER THE À LA MODE

Why the Wright Brothers were successful
- WILBURFORCE

The growth of Communism - REDSPREAD

Shrapnel - PARTICLES OF WAR

Prisoner-of-war camps in Germany in World War II
- STALAGSITES

The Royal Air Force and the Luftwaffe - SKYSCRAPPERS

India's independence from Britain in 1947
- GANDHIWORK

Rubble remaining after the 1967 riot - DETROITUS

Meghan and Harry, recently - WINDSOR NOT

A legend - AFTERMYTH

Monetary Concerns

The Greek goddess of money - PURSEPHONE

Bygone Canadian currency - PAPERBUCKS

Chief Financial Officer - COSTODIAN

How businesses become large - PREMISES, PREMISES

A recession - SLOWBIZ

A deep recession - STUCK MARKET

Being confident about a stock market opportunity
- INVESTITSURE

Twenty cents - DIME AND AGAIN

To search for coins for the parking meter
- QUARTERMUSTER

To spend money on dentures - BUYCUSPIDS

Grocery store receipts - TILL TALES

Driving a rental car - FEEWHEELING

Politics

"We never vote Conservative." - NOTORYUS

Mail-in ballots - POST-IT VOTES

Candidates advocating austerity - CHEAPSLATE

Merely writing letters to protest government policies
- LIMITED SEDITION

The purpose of Trump's border wall - BAN DIEGO

What Trump maintained during the Russia Investigation
- NOCCLUSION

A presidential pardon - CRIME WAIVE

What some political satirists do - RAZZPUTIN

Phonies

The affectation that you're a deep thinker - WISE GUISE

Practising psychoanalysis without a license
- FREUDULENT

A female impersonator - FAKE LOUISE

Sleights of hand - SEEMANTICS

Pretending to be asleep - PSEUDONUMB

A guy who only talks a good fight - SHAMURAI

A prospector panning for gold - SILT SHAKER

Geography

Very close to home - NEXTUS

The back of beyond - NOWHERE REAR

A pretty little stream - BONNYBROOK

A river's path to the sea - SEDIMENTAL JOURNEY

Erosion at work - WEATHERING HEIGHTS

What glaciers do - LANDSCRAPE

The Equator, in Africa - CONGO LINE

Grasslands - HERDQUARTERS

Desert regions - NEVERGLADES

A mine - HOLLOWED GROUND

Aboard a cruise ship - SEAQUESTERED

The Weather

A blizzard - SNOW-IT-ALL

Like very cold weather - WINTERMITTENT

A winter storm in Arizona - SNOWFLUKE

Light breezes - TIDDLYWINDS

The arrival of summer - REJUNERATION

A monsoon - FLOOD DONOR

Sunset - GLOWDOWN

A power outage - LACOLYTES

A Touch of French

Set in Paris - MISE EN SEINE

"Oh, woe is me!" - POOR MOI

"Mon Dieu!" and "Sacre bleu!" - FRENCH CRIES

The lady who brings the tea wagon - CART BLANCHE

A blue blazer - COAT D'AZURE

A lazy afternoon - MATINEE IDLE

She prefers white wine from Germany - MADEMOSELLE

To tear a strip off an employee - FILET MINION

A celebration of lozenges - PASTILLE DAY

He's not the real father - FAUX PA

Movin' On Up

The in-crowd - THEMISPHERE

A class in finishing school - GRACECOURSE

Where debutantes make their entrance - GOWNSTAIRS

Imitating an upper-class voice - ACCENTUAINT

A pretentious manner of speaking - DICTIONAIRY

Place Games

Quebec before 1763 - FRENCH FOREIGN REGION

What Newfoundland has become, unfortunately
- CODFORSAKEN

A place where people might grind their teeth
- GNASHVILLE

A state-run program for better spelling
- PHONICS ARIZONA

The highway median - ROAD ISLAND

The Golden Gate, for example - BRIDGE OF SIZE

Moved to an English county - SUFFOLKATED

England, from the Calais ferry - DOVERSIGHT

Foolish member of the English aristocracy - OLIVER TWIT

Britspeak for "Run as fast as you can!" - LEGITMATE

A Scottish breeze - THISTLEBLOWER

A hat stand for Scots - TAMORACK

Scottish ancestry - MACAROOTS

Scottish scenery - HEATHER AND YON

A guilty Scotsman - HUGHDUNIT

An unsightly Scotsman - GARGYLE

A European guy - ANTON HIM

German melodies - RHINETONES

The telephone book for Prague - CZECHLIST

Place Games, continued.

He speaks Swedish words softly - NORSE WHISPERER

Norwegian neighbour - CLOSE-KNUT

A city I refuse to visit - OSLO, NO WAY

Items made in Helsinki - FINNISH PRODUCTS

Like many Italians - ROMEGROWN

Never growing tired of driving little Italian cars
- INDEFIATIGABLE

Visiting Russia - INBIGNATION

An overworked official in the Russian government
- POLITBURRO

The Russian mint - ROUBLEMAKERS

Putting on airs in Moscow - VLADIDA

A Scottish-Russian guy - PLAIDIMIR

Two close friends - MARGENTINA

Along the route of the Amazon River
- JUNGLE ALL THE WAY

Where you can buy figs at the market - AFGHANISTAND

What children in Iraq might do - NAGHDAD

Where to obtain transportation across the desert
- CAMELLOT

A yurt - TARTAR HOME

An oriental gourmet - EPIKOREAN

Good Looks

Middle Eastern style - CHIC OF ARABY

Beautiful - SEEWORTHY

Stylish moves on the catwalk - DIORSTEPS

High heels - SHOWSHOES

Fast pace in high heels - CLICKETY-SPLIT

Looking good in her new dress - SWISHING WELL

He was so well-dressed, nobody recognized him
- INCOGNEATO

A sparkling diamond - FINGERBLING

Apparel

A cowboy outfit - SPURSUIT

Quite the hat - SOMEBRERO

Velvet golf pants - PLUSH FOURS

His socks need darning - MANIFEST TOES

Winter footwear from Israel - SKIBBUTZ

The opposite of inside-out - UNSEAMLY

Underwear - CLOTHES CLOSEST

Drawers for women's drawers - KNICKERLOCKERS

A certain lady's pair of pants - MARYSCHINOS

Putting on skits - COSTUME FOOLERY

A travelling circus - ANTICS ROADSHOW

Specialists

One who teases - POKESPERSON

A person who wants everything done immediately - PRONTOTYPE

A forensic accountant - ASSET HOUND

Astronauts - MENCAPSULATED

An air traffic controller - BLIPREADER

A regimental padre - MARCHDEACON

A sailor serving beneath the waves - SUBDUDE

Engineers building a bridge - SPANHANDLERS

Slipshod attitude for a bricklayer - LEVEL-MAY-CARE

He nimbly avoids onrushing shoppers - STOREADOR

A witch - HEXPONENT

A person who writes graffiti - NIGHTSCRAWLER

A beachcomber - ALONGSHOREMAN

A demanding boss - CREWDRIVER

A streaker - BAREDEVIL

A demon - HELL-BEING

The Devil himself - HADES MAN

Romance

Casanova - ALPHA ROMEO

Giving her flowers for Valentine's Day - FLEURTATION

Making love in a small boat - CANOEDLING

"Will you marry me?" - PROPOSITIONAL PHRASE

Ready to meet the preacher - INTUXICATED

John and Yoko's marriage - ONOGAMY

A honeymoon suite - LOVE COMPARTMENT

Lovemaking - PREGNANT CAUSE

What led Mother Goose astray - GANDERLUST

A way to break things off - FORGET-ME-NOTE

The end of the affair - FLING WRAP

Christmas

A must-do at Christmas time - CARDTAMOM

"Look—Dad's brought our Christmas tree!" - FIR-FETCHED

Artificial Christmas trees - PINE CLONES

Ghost that visited Ebenezer Scrooge
- CHRISTMAS PRESENCE

Devoted to the Christmas season - YULETIED

Like Santa's workshop - ELF-POSSESSED

Like every chimney on Christmas Eve - SANTASIZED

Santa on Boxing Day - BEATNICK

Naughty - NICE-VERSA

At Home

Mother knows best - MOMNISCIENT

The laundry basket, often - MOTHERLOAD

A man cave - HUBBYHOLE

A nighthawk - LAST ASLEEP

A case of fumbling in the dark - SWITCH HUNT

A neat-freak - DUSTPAIN

What lets you into a room - ISADOOR

"Next time, don't just walk in!" - KNOCK-NEED

Having had no visitors for a very long time - DOORMANT

A very brief agenda - TWO-DO LIST

First thing on the schedule - PRIMA GONNA

"I really need to get this sharpened!" - FUTILITY KNIFE

An item to throw out - NINE-TOOTH COMB

"I'm glad that thing finally got fixed!" - PEACE OF MEND

What shoe polish is for - SCUFFIXES

Scissors - PAIRSNIPS

Sunglasses - SQUINTESSENTIALS

Rural Items

Country living - TRUCK AND FIELD

A poor harvest - MALACROPISM

Corncobs - SHUCK ABSORBERS

A hen's total production - EGGREGATE

A pull on the reins - HORSE ARREST

Just about anything, apparently - GOATMEAL

Where to find wool - ON THE LAMB

The heavy-duty vehicle that you let your brother use
- TRUCKULENT

Tire tracks - HAULMARKS

A Ministry of Agriculture representative
- MAN-AT-FARMS

In Town

A parking space - CURBICLE

A red-light camera, possibly - COLLIDEOSCOPE

A maternity ward - BIRTHDAY SUITE

Graveyards - RESTUARIES

Garrets - LOFTOVERS

The parade route for a championship team - HAILROAD

He's on the way - INTRANSITGENT

What commuter trains do - SHUTTLEBUTT

Whoops!

Ice - SLIPGLOSS

Why it fell over - LEAN-TOO

Why the yacht sank - SLOOPHOLES

To neglect a command - IGNORAMUST

A derailment - DISTRACKTION

Dental troubles - CHOMPLICATIONS

An oil spill - SEASLICKNESS

Incident in the lion's cage - ATEKEEPER

Poorly-planned - ILLRUMINATED

A misspelling in a tattoo - TYPODERMIC

"They've been showing that old movie every week!"
- RERUNDANT

Belly-flops - SPLATFORM DIVING

Why she lost the beauty contest - POORPOISE

Clumsily launching a boat - SLIP-SLIDING AWEIGH

Too many captains - OVERHELMED

An accident candidate - HEEDLESS HORSEMAN

Mishap at the pantry shelf - TINCANDESCENT

Item on the kitchen floor - CRUSTFALLEN

Surprises

Expressions of surprise - EYEFLASHES

She's astounded by almost anything - GOLLYANNA

A loud outburst from a tiny crowd - FEWROAR

The blast of a car horn - EAR JERKER

A hen's squawk - ALARM CLUCK

A salute - RAPID AYE MOVEMENT

Wide of the Mark

To hold on to foolish dreams - FOLLYCODDLE

The illusion that you're brighter than you really are
- HALLUCIDATION

The path to a drunkard's front door - WOBBLESTONES

"Which key is which?" - DISCOMFOBULATED

The inability to distinguish fact from fiction - BULLFOG

Something blown out of proportion
- BIGMENT OF YOUR IMAGINATION

The state of being too dumb to have doubts
- CONFIDENSE

A lack of conviction - STANDIFFISH

Like people at a seance - OPTIMYSTIC

A sword blade that just misses - SKIMITAR

Dancing

What talented dancers have - TWO DEFT FEET

Tap-dancing - SHOEMANSHIP

The polka - WHIRLYJIG

How to waltz, basically - YOU-TURN

Overdoing it on the dance floor - EXAGGYRATING

Hula dancers - GRASSHIPPERS

Bathing

A woman who sings in the shower - SOAPRANO

He sails little boats when he takes a bath - TUBMARINE

His towels are too far away - JACK THE DRIPPER

What happens if you fall asleep in the tub - TEPIDATION

A Jacuzzi for two - BOTHTUB

A shower head - ADJUSTABLE DRENCH

Down the drain - OUT OF SINK

A lake - NATUROBATH

A percussionist's specialty - CYMBALISM

Music

Rosemary's songs - CLOONEY TUNES

Any guitar note in Orbison's "Oh, Pretty Woman"
- CHORDUROY

"Sittin' On the Dock of the Bay" - PIERSPECTIVE

The Rolling Stones' greatest hits - JAGGERNAUTS

"Every Breath You Take" - STING-SONG

Where you can tune in music from Celine Dion
- DIVASTATION

Greatness, to hip-hop fans - EMINEMCE

Descants in hymns - TRILL BITS

A lullaby - NAPTUNE

She sang to her plants, and they all died
- GODDESS OF DISCHORD

A rhythm and blues singer - SOULOIST

Duets - BIVOCALS

A few notes from a symphony - HANDELBARS

An opera singer with no effect on his audience
- PLACEBO DOMINGO

He gave up heavy rock and roll for classical music
- METAL DEFECTOR

A rock concert - NOTHING TO SNOOZE AT

What an unskilled cover band will probably do
- LAME THAT TUNE

Stage and Screen

A distinction for Mulan - SHE SAW BATTLE

Darth Vader, to Luke Skywalker - DADVERSARY

"I am the King of the World!" (line from *Titanic*)
- STATUS QUOTE

Superman in his retirement - EXCAPEIST

Daffy and Donald - STARDUCKS

A common scene in action films - STAIRCHASE

A scary scene in *Jaws* - FINSIGHT

When the commercial is over - BACK TO THE FEATURE

A starring role opposite Marlon Brando
- STELLA PERFORMANCE

Like the cast of *The Bob Newhart Show*
- DOUBLE-DARRYLED

Like Danny DeVito - SHORTBRED

An unknown escape artist - WHOUDINI

Legalities

Eyewitness testimony - CRIME SEEN

People too dumb to realize what they've just seen
- EYEWITLESSES

An unfair trial - COURT-PARTIAL

Judged not guilty of causing an oil spill - EXXONERATED

A gavel - LAW HAMMER

Spoken like a judge - GAVEL-VOICED

Last will and testament - BELEAVEMENT

Inheritance - WILL-GOTTEN GAINS

An unlikely beneficiary in a will - HEIR A PARENT

The O. J. Simpson trial - GLOVE AFFAIR

Shift change at the precinct - COP ROTATION

A subject of recent protests - POLICE DEPORTMENT

Lawlessness

Guilty, like most of us - THICK-SINNED

A false record of payment - DECEIPT

Fraudulent earnings - INCOMEBENT

Money laundering - SCAMOUFLAGE

A Ponzi scheme - SAVINGS BUNK

Like most shady schemes - DUMBFUNDED

What insider traders do - FIDDLESTOCKS

When businesses charge you for every little thing
- MALFEESANCE

A crime scene - ALLEYGORY

A mobster - BIGATONY

How the gangster died - HOLEHEARTEDLY

The victim of a jealous wife - DEADMISTRESS

A getaway vehicle - SCAMPER VAN

A shoplifter - LIGHT-HAND MAN

A dog-napper - DOBERMAN PINCHER

The cops put her in a cell to sober up
- FLORENCE NIGHTINJAIL

What occurs at the auto wrecker's - SAABOTAGE

I wouldn't trust this woman if I were you - DELIELAH

Piracy - THE CRIME OF THE ANCIENT MARINER

A measure of adolescent crime - JUVIE INDEX

Someone who seizes control of your soup - USLURPER

To sneak away without paying your bar bill - TABSCOND

Secretly holding racist viewpoints - KLANDESTINE

To spy on a beach hut - SCOPE A CABANA

Given a dishonourable discharge from the military
- RANKRUPT

Youngsters

A one-year-old - NAPPY DRESSER

A precocious little girl - THINKERBELL

The most annoying child - BRATWORST

Where children should never play - INDISTREET

Grades earned at primary school - KIDMARKS

Wild, like kids at summer camp - RAMBUNKTIOUS

Oldies

An older lady - SENIORITA

People who age well - LOOKKEEPERS

She was a lovely child, but that was many years ago
- OLDILOCKS

He's been in office too long - THE OLD GRAY MAYOR

A bike for senior men - POPSCYCLE

Grandma, at the rifle range - SHOOTENANNY

Granny glasses - RETROSPECS

It happens in my mirror the first thing every morning
- WRECKOGNITION

Positive Outlooks

Optimistic - SUNASSUMING

He has the best of intentions - WOULDSMAN

Quick-witted - SNAPIENT

Sharp - UNOBTUSIVE

Perceptiveness - MINDSIGHT

An extrovert - SHYLACK

To raise a toast - SIP SYNC

At home on the waves - SEACOSY

Positive Talk

Well-spoken words - ARTICULATE MATTER

"Be careful!" - DO DILIGENCE

"Okay, take five." - RESTCUE

"Gimme five!" - HIGHSALUTIN

She's quite the joker - SALLYWAG

Speaking Inuktitut - ARCTICULATION

A reunion is announced - ALLTOGATHER

Lightly chastised - FEATHER-BEATEN

A pulpit in a church - ORAL HIGH GROUND

Negative Talk

A long, boring story - ANECDOZE

To interrupt a conversation - SHEARSAY

A required trait for gossips - SENSE OF RUMOUR

Reply to "Did you hear about Sally?" - SALLYHOO

One who spreads lies - TATTLESNAKE

An app for online gossips - SNYPE

A skilled scold - BLAMETHROWER

He always raises objections - INTERNOPER

"Whatever it is, I'm agin' it!" - DEAFIANT

Giving somebody the bird - CHEEP SHOT

Spiteful language - BITTER PATTER

A tongue-lashing - SCOLD SNAP

A collection of complaints - WHINE LIST

"Oh, quit your griping!" - RESTARANT

To shout an insult and run - HECKLE AND HIDE

A spoilsport - CLOUDSPEAKER

A party pooper's effect - MOOD POISONING

Quite the argument - QUADWRANGLE

A chance to get a word in edgewise - YAPERTURE

Like some persons who express themselves poorly
- YOUSEFUL

The source of complaints in the car - GRUMBLE SEAT

"And what's more . . ." - THATTOO

Crazy talk - NUTTERANCE

"You always use that excuse!" - SAME OLD SORRY

A group of women comparing their aches and pains
- SOREORITY

"Don't squeeze so hard!" - CLAMPLIGHTER

Dire warnings from a foreign power - EPITHREATS

Oil paints and watercolours - EASEL FUEL

Artful (or not)

A feeling of accomplishment - SKILLJOY

An artist's wife - WHISTLER'S OTHER

A scene painted by a cubist - TABLEAU PICASSO

A challenge for a portrait painter
- SUBJECTIVE COMPLEXION

Creating a setting for a diamond - GEMBELLISHMENT

Like origami - FOLD-FASHIONED

A doily - LACEMAT

Knitting - CLICKWORK

A poorly-crafted sculpture - STATUE OF LIMITATIONS

An ugly piece of furniture - DIVAN THE TERRIBLE

Nutritious (or not)

The lineup for burgers - BARBEQUEUE

Stir-fry lovers - SOYALISTS

An entree - CHOW MAIN

Treats for the entire office - BAGAMUFFINS

Very fancy hot chocolate - ROCOCOA

"I prefer orange pekoe." - MEA CUPPA

Spicing up meals - CURRYING FLAVOUR

What carbonated water gives to a soft drink - FIZZASSIST

The food court - MALLNUTRITION

They occupy a worker's mind on the drive home
- DINNERMOST THOUGHTS

"You'll eat it, and you'll like it!" - SUPPERIMPOSED

Inedible - GULLETPROOF

Culinary dismay - AGHASTRONOMY

Burnt potatoes - ASHBROWNS

Insufficiently stirred - UNDERWHIRLED

Leftover lettuce - ROMAINES OF THE DAY

Having one less vegetable in the crisper
- UNENCUCUMBERED

Having eaten too many chocolate marshmallow cookies
- SICKASMORES

Lunch for a fallen woman - WANTON SOUP

Imperfections

Always putting off until tomorrow what he could do today
- SHIRK-INFESTED

A person who is sensitive to criticism - SLIGHTSEER

A spendthrift - EXPENSIEVE

The inability to leave well enough alone - TWEAKNESS

A split personality - FACERIFT

"There's this thing he always does that's really stupid."
- IDIOTSYNCRASY

Acting silly - PUTTIN' ON THE DITZ

One who avoids problems - MUDDLE JUMPER

Anger - BLOODSTEAM

Extremely stubborn - NONBUDGEMENTAL

Upset at not getting a seat - HOTWITHSTANDING

Some people are so crazy it makes me shudder
- LUNATIC CRINGE

A detestable person - LOWWORM

"Where did my energy go?" - SNAPDRAGGIN'

Jumping in feet-first - SHY DIVING

A bumbling buccaneer - PILLAGE IDIOT

To steal a base - SLIDESWIPE

Sports

Acrobatics - TUMBLEDEEDS

A fencing move - COUNTERFEINT

A baseball bat, at times - BUNT INSTRUMENT

What kind of rock is a curling rock?
-TAKE IT FOR GRANITE

Backspin on a golf shot - ROLL REVERSAL

Runners at the starting line - GETSETTERS

Playing defence in football - CONTACT RACING

An unexciting football play - PUNT OF NO RETURN

An easy Nordic cross-country pace - SKIDAWDLE

The odds-on favourite to win at the Olympics
- GOLDCINCH

Having cheered on the winner - RACEHOARSE

Occupying second place - TOPNOT

A shutout - TALLY-NO

The end of a wrestling match - PINCONCLUSIVE

Tom Brady - EXPATRIOT

Muhammad Ali - CHARACTERFISTIC

An unusual auto race - TAXIDERBY

Fan reaction to a goal for the visiting team
- HOMEGROAN

"Aw, c'mon, ref!" - UMPLORE

A comfortable climb for a mountaineer - PEAKEASY

Physical Aspects

Caucasian - TYPEWHITER

Short - CURTALLED

A jutting jaw - CHIN OF COMMAND

A lock of red hair - GINGER SNIP

Heartbeats - TICKERTAPS

A belly laugh - MIRTHQUAKE

A fingerprint database - WHORLPOOL

Muscular - BUFFALOT

To build up strength - DELICATELESSEN

To get used to not taking the elevator - ACCLIMBATIZE

Weight Watchers, Jenny Craig, etc. - DIETTRIBES

To lose pounds successfully - RETURN TO SLENDER

Still overweight - AIN'T THINNER

The length of a person's stride - STEPGAP MEASURE

Taciturn - TONGUE-IN-CHECK

Occupying the Mind

To spend time feeling sorry for yourself - STEWAWAY

What obsessive-compulsive persons do
- HYPERMENTALATE

To obsess about mistakes - BLUNDERFUSS

Worries - REST INHIBITORS

Second thoughts - REPONDERANCE

Déjà vu - SEENERY

A dearest desire - HANKERCHIEF

Different ways of seeking a solution - TRYANGLES

Reliable information - INTELLACTUAL

Training a new employee - HIRE EDUCATION

Knowing when to quit - INTELLIGENT RESIGN

Rubik's cube - PERPLEXITOY

The setting for a chess match - MANEUVERBOARD

A little idea - BRAINDROP

Afflictions

Anxiety - JITTERNESS

An injured person - IN PAIN SIGHT

Serious wounds - MEGAHURTS

Addiction - LACKSTOP

A sob - MOMENTEARILY

A burp - INNERRUPTION

Experiencing nausea - RETCHEDNESS

Sensitive to cold weather - BRRTENDER

Person with a bad cold - DRIPSNORTER

A heavy cold that keeps you in bed - HOME RHEUM

Pollen, perhaps - PESTNASAL

Healing

First aid on the battlefield - MEDIC CARE

A cardiologist - STENT MAN

He treats spasms - TWITCH DOCTOR

A doctor's patients - ILLSORTS

The next person in the waiting room - PATIENT PENDING

A pat on the back - MINIASSURE

A mother comforting her young child - SOOTHESAYER

An attempt to right a wrong - SINSPLINT

46

Substances

A reliable pain reliever - IBUPROVEN

An antidepressant - SAD BLOCKER

Human growth hormone - ACCELERUNT

What tranquilizers tend to do - INERTYA

Caffeine - COFFEE HOP

An energy drink - FLUID BOUNCE

(Same as the above) - VERVE AGENT

Miscellany

How do whisky and brandy taste? - LIQUORISH

Job-seeking - APPLYANCE

The stroke of midnight - LUNATICK

December 31st - YEARSHOT

Acknowledgements

The first person to encounter the entries in this book was my wife, Pat, who heard at least a couple of them most mornings at the breakfast table yet still spoke to me for the rest of the day. I thank her especially for her support at critical moments along the road to the finished product. The idea for the character in the illustrations is hers as well.

Each month during the first two years of the COVID-19 pandemic I sent out some of these puns to my friends Barrie and Gillian Beech, Richard and Bette Kowalczyk, Joan Darby, Don Wright and Al Lightfoot, to my niece Valerie Del Hierro and to my brother Frank Hulme, to offer them a few chuckles. Their encouraging responses provided the impetus for this book. As a group they also vetted the first possibilities for my manuscript, suggesting which ones might be keepers and which might not, and catching factual inaccuracies at the same time. I am very grateful for their help and for being such a considerate audience.

Further thanks go to Richard Cook, who pointed me in the direction of FriesenPress. He told me how helpful and supportive their consultants were during the publishing of his own book, and how professional their experts in editing, formatting, illustrating and printing the book would be. He was certainly right.

CPSIA information can be obtained
at www.ICGtesting.com
Printed in the USA
LVHW020429080423
743511LV00002B/3